FROM GEORGE

A Book of Anecdotes,
Facts and Other Trivia
About Our 41 Presidents

Glenn J. Carpenter
Compiler

TO GEORGE

From George to George

Compiled and published by
Glenn J. Carpenter
948 South Shore Drive
Detroit Lakes, Minnesota 56501
1-218-847-9365

I.S.B.N. 0-911007-26-1

DEDICATION

To my wife, Alice,
whose tireless efforts
made this book possible,

and to my three children,
Kay, Ken, and Karen
who never thought this book
would be published.

Cover Design by

Karen Engebretson
KIE Design
St. Paul, Minnesota

TABLE OF CONTENTS

WHY A BOOK ON PRESIDENTIAL MINUTIAE?

Upon graduation from Hamline University in 1935, I taught American History for nine years. This experience developed in me a keen interest in the story of our country's development and its leaders.

Forty-one men have been elected to the highest office of our land. This fact does not isolate them as a strange, different type of individual. They are real people, as you and I, who enjoyed the same experiences and suffered the same bruises as their constituents.

With this desire to learn more about our presidents, several years ago I began collecting items concerning the lives of our country's most prominent citizens, items with which the average person might not be familiar.

This past year, I decided to publish all of this material. My only hope is that, as the reader peruses these pages, his interest in our presidents will cause him to take a more active interest in our country's history.

Not being an historian, there may be some discrepancies herein, but, for the most part, I think the facts are accurate.

A quote from Bertrand Russell: "There is much pleasure to be gained from useless knowledge."

May you enjoy reading these pages as much as I have enjoyed preparing them!

Glenn Carpenter
May 1992

George Washington
1789-1797

Washington is the only president to have a state named after him.

Washington had an abhorrence of being buried alive, so in his will he specified that his remains should not be buried until three days after his death.

Washington had many hobbies, including cock fights, dancing, fox hunting, horseback riding (considered to be one of the best in the area) the game of poker and gardening.

Although lacking schooling during his youth, Washington conducted his life admirably according to "The Rules of Civility," which consists of 110 rules of decent behavior. This was his guide through life.

At his first inaugural, he set a precedent by adding the words, "So help me God," to the oath of office. He also kissed the Bible where his right hand rested.

Contrary to most history books, Washington was not elected unanimously, since New York State failed to cast its electoral votes.

When Washington took office, the Federal debt was $77,228,000; when he left office it was $79,229,000. The per capita debt at the end of his term was $16.23.

Women participated in his election, because for a period of 5 years the State of New Jersey granted women the vote--132 years before women's suffrage was approved in the Nineteenth Amendment to the Constitution.

Yale historian, Edmund S. Morgan, argues that Washington's genius lay in his understanding of power, both military and political, and in his willingness to use it. He seemed not to have any hunger for personal power. His public demeanor was one of putting great distance between himself and everyone else. He was not on familiar terms with his political or military associates. Mr. Morgan feels that Washington would have been uncomfortable selling himself to the people and would not have been effective on television.

Washington's decision to serve only two terms set a precedent which was followed until the presidency of Franklin D. Roosevelt.

At the time of Washington's death, his financial worth was about one-half million dollars, much of which was in land.

The following is from Washington's will: "It is my express desire that my corpse may be interred in a private manner, without parade or funeral oration." He had a very simple funeral. There were no heads of state in attendance, only the Mayor and Council of Alexandria, neighbors and friends.

In 1789, Washington made a proclamation, naming November 26 a national holiday--Thanksgiving.

Washington is the only president to have been inaugurated in two different cities--New York City and Philadelphia.

Washington's second inaugural speech, delivered March 4, 1793, is the shortest of its kind, only 133 words.

At his death, Washington freed all his slaves, except those who could support themselves or those who wanted to stay. Washington hated slavery, but it was part of the economic system at that time.

General Lafayette once exclaimed that Washington had the largest hands he had ever seen on a human being. His hands were so strong that he could crack a walnut with them. His gloves had to be especially made.

Washington's home at Mt. Vernon consisted of 8,000 acres. It took 200 people to maintain the home and fields.

Washington chose the site of the White House and directed its construction, although he and Martha never lived there.

History does not recognize George Washington as a Republican or Democrat, but as a Federalist.

Washington was a Mason and helped lay the cornerstone of the capitol in Washington, D.C., under the auspices of the Grand Lodge of Maryland.

Vermont, Kentucky, and Tennessee became states during the Washington administration.

John Adams
1797-1801

John Adams and son, John Quincy Adams, are the only father and son presidents, making Abigail Adams the only first lady who was wife and mother to a president.

Mr. and Mrs. John Adams were the first president and wife to live in the White House. Abigail hung their clothing in the now famous East Room.

John Adams is the first of several generations of Adams's, who are considered by many to be the Number 1 family of America. The Adamses produced two presidents and many other brilliant men and women, including this country's brilliant Historian, Henry Adams.

During this period, many people considered the office of Vice-President little more than an errand boy. Of this, Adams said, "My country has in its wisdom contrived for me the most insignificant office that ever the invention of man has contrived or his imagination conceived."

Before President Adams died, he composed a prayer, which, many years later, Franklin Roosevelt had carved on the mantle of the State dining room. It reads: "I pray heaven to bestow the best of blessings on this house and all that shall hereafter inhabit it. May none but honest and wise men ever rule under this roof."

John and Abigail Adams had the longest marriage of any president, 54 years. He has been the only president to live to the age of 90.

Adams was a teacher early in his career, a job which he found boring. He called his small pupils "little runtlings."

Although not known for his wit, the following anecdote is interesting. A Mr. Pinckney accused Adams of bringing four ladies over from England. Adams replied to the charge as follows: "I do declare, upon my honor, if this is true, General Pinckney has kept them all to himself and cheated me out of my two!"

Adams and Washington rarely agreed on anything. However, Adams, being a fair and impartial man, gave an impassioned speech which clinched for Washington the honor of being Commander-in-Chief of the Continental Army.

John Adams and his son, John Quincy Adams, were the only two presidents in the early years of the republic to be denied a second term.

John Adams was the first American to stand before the throne of England.

John Adams was the first president to pose for a camera.

Adams and Jefferson were friends from 1780 throughout Adams' presidency when Jefferson was Secretary of State. An estrangement developed between them, which was perpetuated by followers of each who spread lies about the two gentlemen. After each retired, Adams told a friend, "I always loved Jefferson." When Jefferson heard this, the animosity ended, and they were corresponding with each other until the day of their death--July 4, 1826. Both men died the same day.

Abigail Adams is considered by many historians to have been the best informed lady in the White House, even though she was self taught.   Harry Truman said that she would have been a better president than her husband.

President Adams was considered to be a very heavy smoker. It is said that he started smoking when he was less than ten years old.

Adams admitted that he was not popular, being stubborn, outspoken, impatient, and blunt, with no consideration for the needs of others.

Many consider Adams to be one of our unhappiest presidents.

On the day of his death, Adams last words were, "Jefferson still survives." Little did he know that his friend had died earlier on the same day.

As a member of Congress, John Adams chaired more than 25 committees.

Abigail Adams was often referred to as "Mrs. President" because she was an exceptional woman--very intelligent and self-sufficient.

Thomas Jefferson
1801-1809

Jefferson's many credits include: architect; man of letters; inventor and tinkerer; author and student of the classics; meteorologist, sponsoring the Lewis and Clark expedition; philosopher; statesman; strong advocate of education, founding the University of Virginia.

Jefferson was a very poor manager of money, really his only weakness. Although he was born wealthy, he was in financial straits several times during his life and died bankrupt.

One of Jefferson's many interests was gardening. He grew 250 varieties of vegetables and 150 types of fruit and berries. He travelled around the world in search of seeds.

Jefferson's nickname was "Long Tom," he being six feet, two and one-half inches tall.

Martha and Tom Jefferson had six children, four of whom died at birth. Two daughters, Martha and Maria, survived.

Although Jefferson was not our first Democratic president, he is known as the founder of the Democratic party with its symbol, the donkey.

9

Jefferson was one of two presidents who signed the Declaration of Independence--the other, John Adams.

Jefferson wrote a manual for parliamentary practice which is still the basis for procedure in the Senate of the United States.

Jefferson could be considered the "common man." To show his dislike for some of the customs of the times he refused to wear a white, powdered wig, stating that his red hair was good enough for him. He did away with bowing, shaking hands with visitors in its place. He rode horseback through the streets of Washington. At one time he greeted a royal visitor wearing his old carpet slippers.

Jefferson did not drink hard liquor but enjoyed wine. He was reported to have had a wine bill of $2,800 at one time.

Jefferson was the first president to come to the White House as a widower. During his term of office, Dolly Madison served as his White House hostess.

In 1786, Jefferson was the U. S. Minister to France. He roamed the streets of Paris to buy furniture, damasks, books, paintings, 57 chairs, six mirrors, marble-topped tables, commodes, clocks, glassware, china, even wall paper, for his home at Monticello, which was still in its first phase of construction. In 1795, he redesigned the house, began enlarging it from eight to 21, rooms, adapting many ideas from Parisian architecture. There are many French influences in the Virginia house, including a French portrait of Benjamin Franklin.

During his career, Jefferson never made a political speech, as he was a poor speaker. However, he was an excellent writer and is reported to have answered 1,267 letters in one year. He had invented a poly-graph to make extra copies of his letters.

One of Jefferson's greatest claims to fame was his part in acquiring the Louisiana Territory, which doubled the size of the United States. The purchase was made in 1903 from France at a cost of $16,000,000.

As President, Jefferson's salary was $25,000, which he used to remodel Monticello.

Jefferson brought rice to America from Italy. It was forbidden to export rice under penalty of death, so Jefferson hired a man named Poggio to smuggle rice to Genoa, but he failed. Undaunted, Jefferson stuffed his overcoat pockets with seed and had it delivered to Carolina.

Jefferson's personal library formed the basis for the Library of Congress.

Jefferson was the most gastronomical founding father. He would go to the Georgetown market each morning with his French chef to purchase the produce he wanted. His hospitality kept him broke.

During his second summer in France, Jefferson fell in love with Maria Cosway; however, she was married and the affair became platonic. He had promised his deceased wife, Martha, that he would never marry, a promise which he kept.

Historians claim that Jefferson loved to build and tear down. It took him about 40 years to build Monticello as he continued to add to this splendid home.

During his wife's illness, Jefferson scarcely moved from her bedside. Before she died, she asked him to promise that their children would never have a stepmother. Jefferson promised and kept the promise all his remaining life--44 years.

Jefferson's enemies claimed that if he became president, he would burn all the Bibles in the country. They called him an agnostic and a free thinker. Historians claim this is not accurate; in fact, later in his life he wrote his own Bible, called "The Jefferson Bible."

Following a precedent set by Washington, Jefferson was the second president who chose not to run for a third term.

Jefferson commissioned the Lewis and Clark expedition to explore the vast expanse of land between the Missouri River and the Pacific Ocean.

Jefferson called the presidency, "A Splendid Misery."

In 1826, Jefferson was financially embarrassed. He was given $16,000 by friends, which enabled him to keep his beloved home at Monticello.

Jefferson was the first president to be inaugurated in Washington, D.C.

The three inscriptions on Jefferson's tombstone indicate his choice of his greatest contributions. They are: author of the Declaration of Independence, the Statute of Virginia for religious freedom, and Father of the University of Virginia. He made no mention of his years as president.

On the night of July 3, 1826, Jefferson lay dying and whispered to a friend, "Is this the 4th?" The friend nodded and he fell asleep with a smile on his face.

James Madison
1809-1817

Historians have honored James Madison by calling him "The Father of the Constitution."

With the exception of President Grant, Madison was the smallest president in our history, only five feet tall and weighing at the most 100 pounds. He did not serve in the war as was not able to carry a musket.

Madison never became a member of any church, but he showed a preference for Unitarianism.

Except for his tenure as President, Madison spent his entire life at his home in Montpelier, Virginia--an almost self-sufficient home with its own power plant and police force.

Madison had the only comprehensive notes from the Constitutional Convention. He had his own system of shorthand, taking notes at night and transcribing them during the day. At a later date he was paid $30,000 for these notes, a sum which saved him from financial ruin.

Madison was the first chief executive to serve under fire. During the War of 1812, he hurried from the capitol and went to the battlefield, as the British were very close at Bladensburg, Maryland on August 24, 1813.

The War of 1812 was known as "Madison's War."

In 1814, when the British burned the White House, Dolly Madison saved many historic and valuable items. She had someone unscrew the Stuart portrait of Washington from its frame. With the help of servants, she was able to take four boxes of her husband's papers with her.

Madison devoted much time to the freeing of slaves. He once said to Lafayette, after the Frenchman mentioned that one of his three hobbies was freeing slaves, "Freeing the slaves is almost as dear to me as achieving a union of states." Like other great men of his time, however, Madison owned slaves.

Madison, who had a brilliant mind, completed a four-year course at Princeton in three years. However, he stayed a year longer so he could study Hebrew, as he had intended to enter the ministry.

Dolly Madison had a son by her first marriage to a Mr. Todd. Both she and President Madison barely tolerated the boy, who caused the Madisons much heartache and anguish. Through his spending habits, he was largely responsible for their loss of their wonderful home at Montpelier and to be in poverty until the end of their lives.

Madison generally dressed in black. His servants said the reason for this was that the president could not afford more than one suit.

James Monroe
1817-1825

Monroe was the first president to live in the White House after it was rebuilt following the burning during the War of 1812. The Monroes held a public reception at this time.

The Monroe Doctrine, a warning to European countries to keep their hands off Latin Republics, was named after President Monroe, as it occurred during his administration. The Monroe Doctrine is considered to be the cornerstone of our foreign policy, which exists to this day.

Monroe gave his inaugural address on an elevated "portico" in front of the Capitol. The Speaker of the House, Henry Clay, decided that the floor of the building was not strong enough to hold the many people in attendance. This tradition is still used.

Monroe was the first president to be inaugurated on Monday, March 5, because March 4, the traditional inauguration day, felt on Sunday. He also was the first to be inaugurated out of doors.
Monroe admired his friend, Thomas Jefferson, so much that he moved to Charlottesville, Virginia, to be nearer Monticello. Here he built his home, named "Ash Lawn," with the help of Jefferson.

A friend once asked Monroe if he were not work out while in the Executive Mansion. He replied, "Oh, no! A little flattery will support a man through great fatigue."

In the presidential election of 1820, Monroe fell one vote short of picking up all 232 electoral votes. One elector, William Plumer of New Hampshire, cast his ballot for John Quincy Adams, because he thought that only Washington should have the honor of being elected unanimously.

Monroe was called "The Last of the Cocked Hats," a title indicating that he dressed and acted like an aristocrat. However, in many ways, he was a very ordinary person.

Monroe's wife had lived in France for some time and exhibited it when she, her husband, and children lived in the White House. Mrs. Monroe was a beautiful woman, but was ill much of her life. She was lacking in sociability and refused to make calls or return them. Her daughter served as hostess at the White House when she was ill.

Monroe's daughter, Maria, was the first daughter of a president to be married in the White House--1820.

When Monroe died in New York, he was reported to be $75,000 in debt. His home, "Ash Lawn," was lost. He was originally buried in New York but later moved to Richmond, Virginia, as the people of Virginia wanted him buried in his native state.

John Quincy Adams
1825-1829

John Quincy Adams, who was a member of the Adams family of Braintree, Massachusetts, a political dynasty for more than 100 years, was paranoid about the family name.

John Quincy Adams was a member of the Unitarian Church, as were the other members of the Adams family. He attended church every morning and always read the Bible before retiring, even if there were guests in his home.

Catharine Johnson, wife of John Quincy Adams, was born in England and is our only foreign-born first lady.

John Quincy Adams was largely responsible for the creation of the Smithsonian Institute in Washington, D.C.

John Quincy Adams is the only son of a president to become president himself.

Adams was probably the worst dressed president up to this time. It is said he wore the same hat for 10 years.

John Quincy Adams was graduated from college at 19 years of age. He was a brilliant man but did not become popular until years later. Like his father, he was independent and very honest.

Following his presidency, John Q. Adams, was elected to the House of Representatives seven times by the people of Plymouth, Massachusetts. Because of his many speeches for his causes during this time, he was given the title, "Old Man Eloquent." He was much happier in the House than when he was President.

John Quincy Adams and his wife had a very unhappy marriage; yet they remained together their entire lives.

During Adams' presidency, the expenditures of him and his wife were scrutinized by Congress. Two items questioned were the purchase of a billiard table and a chess set; he reimbursed these expenses.

Adams served in one public office or another through the administrations of eleven presidents.

John Quincy Adams was the only non-partisan candidate in the history of the United States to run for the office of presidency.

Once when Adams was president, he went swimming in the Potomac, leaving his clothes on the bank, where someone stole them. Adams hailed a passing lad and sent him to the White House for a new outfit.

John Q. Adams was delighted, after his stroke in 1846 he returned to his seat in the House with impaired speech and weak, to have all members of the House stand and pay homage to a great man. He died in the speaker's room of the House after his second heart attack.

Andrew Jackson
1829-1837

Although he was conceived as a rough and ready frontiersman, having little education and few graces, in reality President Jackson was a true gentleman and a born leader of men.

Jackson became the first president of the Democratic party. His enemies, the Republicans, used the donkey as the Democratic party symbol in making fun of them.

Jackson had what was known as the first "kitchen cabinet," consisting of his close friends and cronies.

Jackson's home, The Hermitage, located in Nashville, Tennessee, is one of the most famous presidential homes in American history. He and his wife are buried there.

Andrew Jackson was the first president to ride on a railroad train.

In the first-ever assassination attempt against a U.S. President, Jackson was attacked following the funeral of a congressman at the Capitol Building. Fortunately for Jackson, the gun misfired, and Jackson himself subdued the attacker, beating him with his cane.

Because of Jackson's toughness, his fighting men referred to him as "Old Hickory."

Jackson's inauguration was the wildest in history, with much drinking, breaking of furniture, etc. At one time the President was pinned to the wall by the crowd and he had to make his escape with the help of friends.

Jackson and Rachel lived as man and wife for two years without being legally married. Rachel had been married to a Mr. Robards, who, she thought, had secured a divorce but hadn't done so. The two were then married again, but the situation caused the Jackson's trouble the rest of their lives. Jackson, with his uncontrollable temper, would challenge anyone who alluded to the affair in a demeaning way.

His wife, Rachel, died a short time before her husband was to be inaugurated. Her niece, Mrs. Emily Donelson, became the White House hostess.

Both Jackson and his wife smoked corncob pipes.

At the conclusion of his presidency when Jackson headed for his home, The Hermitage, he was a sick, sad, and poor man, having only about $100 in cash on his person. His home was heavily mortgaged due to the debts of his adopted son.

Jackson's funeral was the largest in history. Thousands of friends choked the road so that they could pay their respects to one of our great leaders.

Martin Van Buren
1837-1841

Van Buren began studying law, first in his home town, Kinderhook, then in New York City. In 1820 he was admitted to the bar when he was 20 and began his law practice in Kinderhook.

Van Buren became president in 1836 on Andrew Jackson's coattails. Seven weeks following his inauguration, he ran pell mell into our first real panic. Van Buren was blamed, but Jackson was the culprit because of his banking policy.

Van Buren was nicknamed "Old Kinderhook," after his birthplace. His New York City supporters formed the O.K. Club. "O.K.!" became a rallying cry for the Democrats and is now the most widely used word in America.

Van Buren was the first president to have been born an American citizen, rather than a British subject.

Van Buren was the first president to have a bathtub in the White House.

Although Van Buren was considered an office holder with talents for intrigue and leadership, these qualities did not make his presidency noteworthy because he could not separate himself from the controversial policies of his predecessor, Andrew Jackson.

Van Buren was considered to be an elegant dresser, a dapper person whom some called a "fop." His enemies accused him of eating his meals on fancy plates, drinking wine from silver coolers, and other extravagances, such as installing a hot water tank in the White House to warm his bath water.

The campaign of 1840, which Van Buren lost, was the first one to experience fraudulent voting.

Van Buren was called "The Little Magician" by his friends and "The Red Fox of Kinderhook" by his enemies. An astute politician, he mastered the art of politics like a painter would master his art.

Men who came to the White House seeking employment were personally greeted by President Van Buren, as he would not leave this job to his assistants.

Within a period of 12 years, Van Buren held the following offices: U.S. Senator, Secretary of State, Vice-President, and President.

His principal accomplishment was the establishment of the National Treasury and regional subtreasuries for the control of the currency.

President Van Buren was very feeble before he left office, with his hearing and sight failing. At one of his last receptions, he was so weak that he couldn't stand, but sat to greet his guests.

William Henry Harrison
1841

Harrison had the shortest term of any president, as he died 31 days after taking office. At his inauguration, he defied precedent and a blinding rainfall and led the inaugural parade on horseback. He wore neither a hat or coat, resulting in a cold which led briskly to pneumonia, the cause of his death.

Harrison was the first president to arrive in Washington, D.C., by train for his inauguration. He registered at the Cadsby Hotel, one of the most popular at this time.

Harrison's inaugural address consisted of 8,578 words, took one hour and forty-five minutes to deliver, and was the longest in history.

When he took office, Harrison was our oldest president, 68 years and 23 days. Because of his age, he was called "Granny" throughout the campaign of 1840.

William Harrison was the first president to have his photograph taken in office.

William Harrison was called "General Mum," because he was told to avoid bringing issues into the colorful campaign of 1848, which was devoid of issues and policies.

Harrison and his wife, Anna, had ten children, five of whom died at an early age. Anna did not want her husband to go to Washington, sending her daughter-in-law in her place. Anna was in poor health; when her husband became president, she went to North Bend, Ohio, where she died 20 years later, never having seen her husband after he went to Washington.

Singing was popular during Harrison's campaign; one of the most popular songs was "Yankee Doodle," sung in particular by the Whig party of whom Harrison was a candidate. He was the first member of this party to be elected president.

More people voted in Harrison's election than ever before--2 1/2 million votes were cast. He was the only president to campaign for himself.

Harrison is the only president in our history who studied to be a doctor. Instead of becoming a doctor, he became a professional soldier.

Harrison was not a poor man when he ran for president, but his followers depicted him as a person who lived in a log cabin and drank hard cider. In fact, his campaign was called "the hard cider campaign," a slogan being "Keep the ball rolling."

Harrison was our first president to lie in state in the White House.

Harrison was the second president whose father had been a signer of the Declaration of Independence.

John Tyler
1841-1845

Tyler was the first president to be called an "accidental" president. He took the office of president, following the death of William Harrison.

Tyler was the first president to be married in the White House.

Tyler, who had two wives, holds the record for having had the most children--15. His first wife, Letitia, bore him eight children and died during the last two years of her husband's term of office. After a short courtship, Tyler married Julia Gardner, daughter of a wealthy family and twenty years younger than Tyler. She bore him seven children. Tyler was 70 years old when he fathered his last child.

Congress thought so little of Tyler that they would not allow him money for maintenance of the White House.

On the last day of his term of office, Tyler became the first president to have a veto overridden by Congress.

Tyler and his children span almost the entire period of American history, inasmuch as he was born during Washington's administration, and his youngest child died when Harry Truman was president.

Tyler was the only president to change party in midterm. Sponsored for office by the Whigs, he defied his party's policies and became a virtual Democrat shortly after assuming office.

Tyler was the first president whose wife died while he was in office.

When Tyler's horse, "The General," died, the President had him buried at his Virginia home, with this inscription over the grave: "Here lies the body of my good horse, The General. For twenty years he bore me around the circuit of my practice, and in all that time, he never made a blunder. Would that his master could say the same."

Tyler experienced many problems as president; one was caused by his having had no party affiliation. Another was his feud with Henry Clay, resulting in the resignation of all cabinet members, except for Daniel Webster.

One of Tyler's greatest achievements was the annexation of Texas.

Letitia Tyler, grand-daughter of President Tyler, was the first girl born in the White House. Her parents were Tyler's son, Robert, and his wife, Priscilla.

On January 18, 1862, his death was completely ignored by the American press, public, and government for, by then he had become a congressman of the enemy Confederate States of America.

James Knox Polk
1845-1849

Polk was little-known as a candidate for the presidency, becoming our first "dark horse candidate."

Polk thoroughly disliked social functions and once said, "I cannot lose half a day just to go dining."   He was a workaholic and many historians consider him the hardest working president in our history.

Mrs. Polk was a member of a Moravian religious group and forbad gaiety in the White House. This included dancing, playing cards, and consumption of alcoholic beverages. She also refused to attend the theater and horse racing and would not talk to strangers on the Sabbath.

Under President Polk, the United States issued its first postage stamp. Pictures of Benjamin Franklin and George Washington were used.

At his inaugural, Polk presented his wife, Sarah, a fan decorated with pictures of all the presidents who preceded him. On the reverse side of the fan was a picture of the signing of the Declaration of Independence.

During one term, Polk established the Department of the Interior, the Smithsonian Institute, and the Naval Academy.

The most important features of Polk's administration were the reception of Iowa and Wisconsin into the Union, reduction of the tariff, acquisition of California and New Mexico from Mexico for a bargain $15 million, and settlement of the Oregon boundary dispute with England ("fifty-four, forty, or fight".)

One of Polk's campaign slogans was "the reannexation of Texas and the reoccupation of Oregon." Oregon was coupled with Texas in order to gain Northern support for westward expansion. After Polk's victory, but before he took office, a joint resolution inviting Texas to join the Union was passed by Congress. President Tyler signed it on March 1, 1845, 3 days before Polk's inauguration.

Sarah Childress Polk was the first president's wife to serve as her husband's secretary.

James Polk was salutatorian of his class at the University of North Carolina. He was a short man with an excellent speaking ability. Because of these two qualities, he was nicknamed, "Napoleon of the Stump." He was also called "Young Hickory," as he was a protege of Andrew Jackson.

During Polk's administration, the first gas lights were installed in the White House, replacing the old lamps.

When Polk and his wife left the White House, they both agreed the feeling was "like Christmas."

Mrs. Polk lived 42 years after her husband's death. During that time, she never left her home except to attend church.

Zachary Taylor
1849-1850

Taylor was the first president elected to the office with no previous political experience. Because he was a national hero and a blustering, boasting general, he was nominated for the presidency by the Whigs in 1848.

Taylor's physical features were anything but attractive. His legs were so short that he had to be hoisted onto his horse, and when there, preferred to ride side-saddle with both legs dangling on the same side of the animal. However, he was tough, self-reliant, and self-sufficient.

The letter informing Mr. Taylor of his nomination to the presidency arrived "10 cents due," which he refused to pay and destroyed the letter. A messenger later informed him of his nomination.

It is said Taylor's wife, Margaret, prayed that her husband not be nominated for the presidency. She felt his nomination was a plot to deprive her of his society and shorten his life. After less than a year and a half in office, Taylor died.

Strange as it may seem, Taylor chose his own cabinet but didn't know any of them personally. His entire cabinet consisted of lawyers and House or Senate members.

During the Mexican War, Zachary Taylor, known as "Old Rough and Ready," and General Winfield Scott, known as "Old Fuss and Feathers," were on the same side. By the time the war was over, both were national heroes. As a result, the two generals took opposite sides, each seeking the presidential nomination at the Whig Party Convention. In the battle of the Whig Convention, "Old Rough and Ready" defeated "Old Fuss and Feathers."

President Taylor's daughter, Knox, became the bride of Jefferson Davis, who later became president of the Confederate States of America. Davis remained a widower many years after her untimely death. The President always considered Davis as family, even after his remarriage.

When President Taylor became annoyed with presidential problems, he got away from it all by saddling up "Whitey," his favorite cavalry horse, whom he kept pastured on the White House lawn. These rapid gallops around Washington tended to soothe the intense anger of the President.

On July 4, 1850, President Taylor attended official ceremonies in Washington. It was a very warm day, and he overate sliced cucumbers and drank much iced milk. He became very ill and died in the White House on July 9, only sixteen months after taking office.

At his funeral, about 100 carriages formed a two-mile procession accompanying the body of the war hero and President to his grave.

Millard Fillmore
1850-1853

Fillmore was not an effective president; his accomplishments were said to be secondary to his good looks. He probably never would have been president, except for the death of President Taylor.

Up to this time in our history, Fillmore was the only vice-president to succeed to the presidency. All of Taylor's cabinet resigned, and Fillmore formed a new one.

Fillmore enjoyed the first bathtub in the White House, installed in 1850. It was large, lined with zinc and mahogany. It served the next six administrations.

Fillmore's wife, Abigail, a former teacher of the president, was responsible for two significant innovations: she urged her husband to get Congress to grant an appropriation for the first library in the White House; she was instrumental in having the first iron stove installed in the kitchen, replacing open fire cooking. Because of its complexity, the President had to visit the Patent Office to see how the stove worked.

Fillmore's attire drew attention to him as he always wore a dark, frock cloak, a high-collared shirt with a black silk neck cloth tied in a bow.

In those days a person who failed to pay his debts could be sent to prison. President Fillmore had an act passed which did away with this law.

Never a well-known president, before or after his term of office, a group of people created an organization called the Baltimore-based Society to Promote Respect and Recognition of Millard Fillmore. Every January 7, Fillmore's birthday, a party is given in his honor; invitations are extended to prominent politicians, but in seven years, no one has accepted.

Fillmore's will directed his executors "to destroy all correspondence to or from my father, mother, or me." However, Charles D. Marshall, an executor, preserved many papers which were stored away and did not appear until 1969. A count revealed the existence of over 10,000 documents, whose contents have yet to be revealed.

Millard Fillmore was not an incumbent defeated for reelection in 1852, as he was not given the nomination that year by his party.

After the disintegration of the Whig Party in 1850, Fillmore refused to join the Republican Party and in 1856 accepted the nomination for president of the Know Nothing or American Party. Other unsuccessful parties with whom he became affiliated were the Anti-Catholic Party, the Star-Spangled Banner Party, and the Anti-Mason Party. None of these actions improved his place in history.

Franklin Pierce
1853-1857

Pierce was the youngest person to be elected President up to that time. He was 49 when elected.

Franklin Pierce, the good-looking, friendly "dark horse" from New Hampshire, became the 14th president at a time when America was hopelessly divided over the slavery issue. His term of office would have been stressful to the greatest of men.

As a military man, he fainted twice during battle, once when his horse threw him. After the second incident, he was considered a coward; however, he had a good military record.

The Pierce's lost two sons when they were very young. Later, the only living child, Benjamin, was killed in a train derailment, the parents suffering only minor injuries. Mrs. Pierce never recovered from the loss of her son. In her grief, she was said to have written letters to her dead children. Benjamin's death occurred only two months before his father's inauguration.

Pierce was the first President to have a Christmas tree in the White House.

When Mr. Pierce was in Congress, his wife, Jane, had such a dislike of Washington that her husband resigned from Congress and they returned home. By the same token, she was displeased when he was elected president.

The White House green house was built during his administration, which lead to the tradition of fresh-cut flowers daily in the White House.

Pierce was an excellent speaker and delivered his inaugural speech entirely from memory.

Pierce may have been the most handsome president, with black curly hair. He had the nickname of "handsome Frank." However, his temperament prevented him from become a great statesman at that time.

The United States held its first World's Fair under Pierce's administration.

Central heating was installed in the White House in 1853 during Pierce's administration.

In today's presidential oath are the words, "I do solemnly swear...,." Pierce used the word "affirm" instead of "swear."

Franklin Pierce was a graduate of Bowdoin College, Brunswick, Maine. Among his classmates and friends were Henry Wadsworth Longfellow and Nathaniel Hawthorne, the latter assisting the President in the writing of his speeches.

James Buchanan
1857-1861

Buchanan was the first elected president who was not a British subject.

Buchanan was our only bachelor president. Early in his career he was engaged to Anne Coleman, the daughter of wealthy parents, who did not want their daughter to marry Buchanan, since they felt he was marrying her for her wealth. She moved away and died at an early age, with some hint of suicide. Buchanan was refused permission to attend her funeral.

Buchanan was a very cautious man when it came to money and acquired the nickname of "Old Buck."

President Buchanan was near-sighted in one eye and far-sighted in the other. Consequently, he was always seen with his head tilted to one side.

Buchanan was the first president to have his photograph taken with his entire cabinet.

Considered to be one of our least successful presidents, Buchanan seemed unable to confront problems. Because he was 65 when he was inaugurated, many felt he was too tired and old to be an effective president.

Buchanan adopted his sister's daughter, Harriet Lane, who accompanied him to London when he served as Ambassador. When he was elected President, she served as his hostess in the White House. She was well educated, a fine painter, and a style setter.

Buchanan was Secretary of State under President Polk, who was not too friendly because he feared that Buchanan had ambitions to be president. Buchanan said of his superior, "My life is that of a galley slave. "President Polk said of Buchanan: "Mr. Buchanan is an able man, but is in small matters without judgment and sometimes acts like an old maid."

During his administration, with the help of Harriet Lane, his niece and hostess, they entertained the Prince of Wales, later to become George VII. A new song was introduced at this gathering entitled, "Listen to the Mocking Bird."

James Buchanan was the first president to be expelled from college. In 1808 he was dismissed from Dickinson College for disorderly conduct.

Buchanan was nicknamed "Ten-Cent Jimmy" because he strongly advocated imposing low tariffs on goods and offering low wages to workers.

At his death, Buchanan had a fortune estimated at $300,000, which he had earned through careful business habits and his successful law practice.

Abraham Lincoln 1861-1865

The tallest of our presidents, Lincoln, was six feet, four inches in height and weighed about 180 pounds. His unruly hair and stooped posture gave him a rugged appearance.

Lincoln was a Mississippi steamboat pilot at age 23. A year later he and a partner bought and ran a saloon. He also worked as a postmaster and flatboat pilot.

Lincoln was a champion wood-splitter; it was said he could do the work of three men.

Lincoln's Secretary of State, William H. Seward, accepted the cabinet post when offered by the President because he looked upon Lincoln as somewhat of a "country bumpkin" whom he could dominate without much effort.

Lincoln was a religious man but had no affiliation with any one church. It is said he attended worship services regularly.

Mrs. Lincoln had a passionate desire to become Washington's society leader; because of this she spent large sums of money, particularly on clothing. For instance, it is said that she bought 399 pair of gloves. Her debts for clothing amounted to $27,000. Despite her extravagance in her dress, she was really a pinch penny in all other regards.

Lincoln was the first president to be photographed at his inauguration.

Lincoln was an excellent story teller; for example, when he lost the Senate seat to Douglas, he said, "I feel just like the little boy who stubbed his toe--too big to cry and it hurts too much to laugh.

Mary Todd came from a family with good standing in the community; she had charm and was quite a belle. She had been courted by Stephen Douglas and John C. Breckenridge, as well as Lincoln. Her courtship with Lincoln was a tumultuous and hectic one, but they eventually married and had four children. Only Robert survived to maturity.

After his election, Lincoln and associates heard that there would be an attempt on the President's life; as a result, he bypassed Baltimore on his way to Washington. He was disguised as an invalid in a Pullman berth on this secret journey.

For most o# her life, Mrs. Lincoln suffered from deep depression, caused primarily by the deaths of their three sons. Following the death of Willie, she never again entered his room. In later years, her mind gave way following Lincoln's death and at the time, she was judged to be insane. However, later she was declared competent.

At the surrender of Lee at Appomattox, President Lincoln had the band play "Dixie," as he said it was one of the best tunes he had ever heard and "now we have captured it."

Lincoln established Thanksgiving as a national holiday in 1863.

Lincoln was the first president to wear a beard. Eleven-year-old Grace Bedell of Westfield, New York, is said to have written him the following in 1860: "....you would look a great deal better for your face is so thin. All the ladies like whiskers and they would tease their husbands to vote for you." By March, 1861, when he reached Washington, D.C., for his inauguration, Lincoln had a beard.

A Mr. Charles Dresser, the minister who married Mary Todd and Abraham Lincoln, later sold the Lincoln's his house in Springfield for $1,500. The house is now an historic site and attracts many visitors.

Lincoln was the first president to have his portrait on a coin--the Lincoln penny, 1809.

Lincoln almost canceled his trip to Gettysburg, due to his general poor health and exhaustion. After his speech, he spent three weeks recuperating; some say that he had smallpox.

At Lincoln's inauguration, there were three persons present who would later become presidents: Garfield, Benjamin Harrison, and Rutherford B. Hayes.

Although the famous East Room of the White House was used for many functions during Lincoln's presidency, it was used to house Union soldiers during the war.

In March, 1865, Lincoln dreamed of his own death. It is said he went to the East Room and saw soldiers guarding the body of a man who was stretched out on a table. Lincoln asked what had happened and the soldiers said the President had been assassinated. Four days later, the President was shot by John Wilkes Booth at Ford's theater.

Lincoln's speech at Gettysburg took only two minutes to deliver. When the speech was over, Lincoln declared to friends that it was a failure; some even called it "silly." The speech had just ten sentences, 271 words, 202 of which were just one syllable. It took many years for it to take its rightful place in history.

Lincoln's final resting place is in his tomb at Oakridge Cemetery, Springfield, Illinois. His body is buried in a vault ten feet below ground, made of steel and concrete, hermetically sealed and topped with twenty inches of concrete. All of the Lincoln family, except

Robert, are buried here. Since Robert's life was spent in government service, he was buried in Arlington Cemetery.

After his death, Lincoln was the first president to lie in state in the rotunda of the Capitol.

Famous quotes from President Lincoln: "My father taught me to work; he did not teach me to love it." Of his mother, Nancy Hanks, "All that I am and hope to be, I owe to my loving mother." "I have been driven many times to my knees by the overpowering conviction that I had no where else to go. My own wisdom and that of all about me seemed insufficient for the day." "The ballot is stronger than the bullet."

Andrew Johnson
1865-1869

Johnson is our only President who never attended school. His wife, Eliza McCardle, who was only 16 when they were married, taught her husband how to read and write and helped him to become a good speaker.

Andrew Johnson and his brother were indentured servants of a tailor in Raleigh, North Carolina. Such a servant was bound by a contract to work for a master for the term of the contract. Andrew broke a window in the tailor shop and the two brothers ran away. The owner posted a $10 reward for the capture of Andrew which was never collected.

Realizing the importance of education because of his lack of it, he established the first public school in Tennessee.

Resenting anything controversial or degrading that was said about working people, due to his own early life, Johnson said, "Don't forget that Adam was a tailor and our Saviour was the son of a carpenter.

President Johnson was tried for impeachment with what now are considered questionable charges. Johnson did not appear at the trial, which lasted more than two months. 35 Senators voted for impeachment and 19 voted for acquittal, one vote short of the 2/3 majority required. Johnson is our only President to be tried for impeachment.

The most valuable achievement of Johnson's term in office was the purchase of Alaska for $7,200,000. At that time people referred to the purchase as Seward's (Secretary of State) Folly and Johnson's Polar Bear Garden.

Johnson was 19 when he became a father for the first time.

In 1866, Andrew Johnson became the first President to receive the visit of a Queen--Queen Emma of the Sandwich Islands, now Hawaii.

Johnson was the first person to take a seat in the Senate after being out of the presidency for six years, the only ex-president to be elected to the Senate. In spite of his impeachment hearings, he found his desk in the Senate Chamber covered with flowers and he was given a standing ovation by Senate members.

Johnson was only briefly a senator, suffering a stroke at the Tennessee home of his daughter and died on July 31, 1875. His burial place is a hilltop outside Greenville, Tennessee. He was buried with a flag and a copy of the Constitution.

As he was an ardent admirer of Jefferson and Jackson, Johnson was a Democrat but not a faithful party man, feeling that the needs of the people came first.

Ulysses S. Grant
1869-1877

At birth Grant was named Hiram Ulysses Grant; later he changed it to "Ulysses Hiram Grant," to avoid the initials that spelled "HUG." Through the help of a Congressman, he received an appointment to West Point; the Congressman mistakenly thought his middle name was "Simpson," his mother's maiden name. He remained Ulysses S. Grant: for his entire life.

Grant's reputation as a drinker harmed him in many instances. According to the New York Herald, November 26, 1863, a group of clergymen visited President Lincoln, saying that General Grant was an unsafe leader because of his drinking. Lincoln, the story goes, replied with a twinkle in his eye, "So General Grant drinks? Well, I wish some of you would tell me the brand of whisky he drinks. I would like to send a barrel of it to every one of my generals."

Grant was the first president to graduate from a United States Military Academy.

In seven years Grant rose from a salaried job of $800 annually to the President of the United States.

A magnificent act of General Grant's followed Lee's surrender at the Appomattox Courthouse. Lee asked Grant if his men and officers would be allowed to keep their horses. Grant replied, "Have all of them take their horses, enlisted men and officers as well. They will need them for spring plowing."

President Grant's wife, Julia, was cross-eyed. She wanted to have a newly-developed operation to uncross her eyes, but her husband refused, saying "I like her that way."

Grant knew next to nothing about handling money. Following a drunken incident when his commanding officer threatened to court martial him or he could resign, he chose the latter. He took his family back to the Midwest, tried farming, real estate, store keeper, and failed at all of them. The Civil War rescued him from economic mediocrity and turned him into a national hero.

Following his terms as president, Grant was heavily in debt and afflicted with cancer. In order to leave his wife, Julia, some financial assistance he started to write his memoirs with the help of Mark Twain. The document entitled, THE PERSONAL MEMOIRS OF U. S. GRANT, consisted of two volumes, over 1,200 pages, and nearly 300,000 words. His literary work was completed just before his death and sold for around $500,000.

Grant gave up a guaranteed income for life when he resigned from the Army to become President. No President shared Grant's fate of dying destitute.

A Union officer once asked Lincoln to replace Grant, who at the time was not doing too well. Lincoln refused, saying, "I can't spare the men because he fights."

Rutherford B. Hayes
1877-1881

President Hayes was considered to be one of the most honest, straight-forward, and congenial of all presidents. Because of these qualities, other candidates allowed the presidential convention to be held in Hayes' home state of Ohio.

Hayes won the election of 1876 from Samuel Tilden in what was the most controversial election up to that time. Hayes won by only one vote, after Tilden had earlier been pronounced the winner.

Both President and Mrs. Hayes were considered to be the most devout and religious of all presidential families. They read a chapter from the Bible at breakfast each morning.

President Hayes felt that women were a great influence on man and his inspiration. However, he was not an advocate of women's rights and was opposed to allowing women to vote.

Mrs. Hayes was the first wife of a president to be called "First Lady."

Mrs. Hayes would allow no liquor or smoking in the White House, for which she was severely criticized. She was given the name of "Lemonade Lucy." One of her reasons for not serving liquor was that she wanted the Republican Party to keep the temperance movement alive.

President Hayes took more pride in being a former commander of his 23rd regiment of Ohio volunteers than he did in being President of the United States.

Hayes was an excellent soldier who craved action; he was wounded five times.

Hayes took a private oath of office on Saturday, March 3, as the usual inaugural date fell on a Sunday. He took a public oath on Monday, March 5, before 3,000 people on the Capitol steps.

President Hayes' attire seldom varied--a silk hat, frock coat, black pants, and black shoes. He was short of stature and wore a beard that some say looked like a "rat's nest."

Lucy Hayes was the first president's wife to hold a degree from an accredited college.

When Congress banned the traditional Easter Monday egg-rolling festivities on the grounds of the Capitol Building, Lucy Hayes promptly invited the children of Washington to enjoy the occasion on the White House lawn, where it has been held ever since.

Lucy died suddenly at the age of 57. Less than four years later, after a visit to her grave, Hayes said, "My feeling was one of longing to be quietly resting in a grave by her side." He died nine days later.

James A. Garfield
1881

Garfield was the first president to attend his own nomination for office.

Mrs. Eliza Garfield was the first mother to attend her son's inauguration.

Garfield was our first left-handed president. He was also ambidextrous and could write Greek and Latin at the same time, using both hands.

Garfield was one of our "front porch" candidates, because he did not travel during his campaign but gave his speeches from his home.

Garfield's talent for teaching was discovered while working as a custodian at Hiram College. After receiving a degree from Williams College, he returned to Hiram as professor of classical languages. In 1857 he became president of Hiram College.

At the age of 31, Garfield became one of the youngest generals in the Union Army.

His military career was unusually successful, which brought him to the attention of the Ohio Republican party. He resigned from the army in December, 1863, and began an outstanding 18-year career as a Congressman.

Garfield was the first president to use a telephone.

Garfield became a fine preacher. He was impressive because of his good looks, six-foot frame, and broad shoulders. He had been courting Lucretia Rudolph since childhood, and his preaching was largely responsible for her consenting to marry him.

Garfield was the second of our presidents to be assassinated after having served only 200 days of his term of office. During 80 of those days, he lay near death.

In July, 1881, while in the Washington railroad station, prior to a trip to Williams College, a disappointed office seeker approached the area from behind and shot the President twice, the second shot lodging in Garfield's back. He was hospitalized for two months, doctors futilely trying to extract the bullet. Garfield finally asked to be taken to the seashore, where he died September 19, 1881.

Dr. Alexander Graham Bell, inventor of the telephone, was asked to use his induction balance electrical device to try to find the location of the bullet, but he was unsuccessful.

Eliza Garfield was the first President's mother to live in the White House with her son and daughter-in-law.

Garfield's final words were, "My work is done."

Chester Arthur
1881-1885

Arthur became President seven months after being elected to the office of the Vice-President, following President Garfield's death. Americans knew little of Arthur and were filled with anxiety over his presidency.

As a struggling young lawyer in New York City, he gained public attention by defending a negro woman who had been removed from a street car in Brooklyn because of her race. Arthur won $500 in damages for his client.

Arthur was one of the most handsome presidents, tall, with side whiskers and full mustache, dark hair, and brown eyes. In fact, some mistook him for an actor.

Arthur was always well dressed--a Prince Albert coat with a flower in the button hole--a very well known person in Manhattan society, he loved fine clothes, good food, and to entertain friends. He was the first President to employ a valet, which was frowned upon at that time.

Arthur took the oath of office for the presidency twice following the death of President Garfield, in New York on September 20, 1881, and again two days later in the Capitol.

When Arthur took office, he was very dissatisfied with the White House furnishings. He said he would not live there if changes were not made. He had a huge auction, disposing of 24 wagon loads of furniture and other items. The mansion was eventually redone in Mid-Victorian style.

Some of the items sold by Arthur from the White House attic dated back to the time of our second President, John Adams. A copy of Lincoln's inaugural address and Abigail Adams' trunk were among the items.

In 1859 Arthur married Ellen Lewis Herndon of New York City. The couple had two sons and one daughter. Mrs. Arthur died the year in which her husband was elected Vice-President.

President Arthur's youngest sister, Mary Arthur McElroy, served as hostess of the White House and took care of his motherless daughter. Mrs. McElroy began the custom of serving tea to the many guests who were at the White House for public receptions.

President Arthur was regarded as the finest fisherman in the country. He fished for salmon, trout, and striped bass. He caught an 80 lb. bass off the coast of Rhode Island.

Mark Twain said of Arthur's presidency: "I am but one...still in the opinion of this one...it would be hard to better President Arthur's administration."

Grover Cleveland
1885-1889

Grover Cleveland is the only president elected to two non-consecutive terms.

Cleveland paid a 32-year old illiterate to serve as a substitute for him in the Union Army. At this time in history, this was done quite frequently. Cleveland's reason for not joining the Army was that he felt he needed to take care of his mother and sister. His two brothers were all ready serving in the armed forces.

During his campaign for president and before he was married, Cleveland admitted that he had fathered a child of a lady of bad reputation. When his friends asked him what he was going to do a-bout it, he replied, "Tell the truth." Evidently, people believed him, as he won the election in spite of the gossip.

Cleveland was a very heavy man; as a president, he was second in weight only to William Taft. His weight was 250 pounds, prompting his relatives to call him "Uncle Jumbo."

Cleveland was the first president to be married in the White House. He married Frances Folson, 20 years younger than he, the daughter of his former law partner, and for whom he had served as guardian. Their daughter was the first girl to be born in the White House.

Mrs. Cleveland was the youngest hostess of the White House.

During his campaign for president and as a result of his admission to having fathered an illegitimate child, the following was composed: "Ma! Ma! Where's my Pa? Gone to the White House! Ha! Ha! Ha!"

When Cleveland lost the election following his first term, Mrs. Cleveland informed the servants that she and her husband would be back and they should not disturb the furniture, etc. She was correct-- they returned.

Cleveland was the president who dedicated the Statue of Liberty.

John Phillip Sousa played the wedding march at Cleveland's marriage.

Famous quotations attributed to Cleveland: "Man has never made a structure that could outlive a book." "I have tried so hard to be right." "A public office is a public trust."

Cleveland often answered the telephone himself during his first term, as he had a weakness of not being able to delegate responsibility.

Cleveland served during the 49th, 50th, 53rd, and 54th terms of Congress.

Benjamin Harrison
1889-1893

Harrison was inaugurated 100 years after the inauguration of our first president, George Washington.

Benjamin Harrison proudly wore the hat of his grandfather and former president, William Henry Harrison. When he ran for president, many made fun of him saying that the hat was too big for him. By the way, he was one of the shortest presidents, 5 ft. 6 inches.

When electricity was installed in the White House, the Harrisons were so cautious about touching the lights that they often left them burn all night. The servants would turn them off in the morning.

Six states entered the union during Harrison's presidency, more than any other administration.

Harrison's wife, Caroline, was the first president of the Daughters of the American Revolution.

The Harrison family prayers lasted at least a half hour.

When the Harrisons' moved into the White House, they enjoyed the luxury of a bath tub; however, it had to accommodate eleven persons.

Harrison's great grandfather was one of the signers of the Declaration of Independence.

President Harrison was the last president to wear a beard.

The Harrisons changed some White House customs, bringing back dancing, after the Polk administration disallowed it.

The custom of flying the United States flag over public buildings was begun during the Harrison term.

The Harrisons were granted money by Congress to renovate the White House and install electricity. During this process, old cupboards and shelves were found which held pieces of crystal and china from other administrations. Mrs. Harrison started the White House china collection with this material.

The Harrisons were the first presidential family to have a Christmas tree in the White House.

During Harrison's administration, Congress appropriated a billion dollars--the first time except in war.

After leaving the White House, President Harrison said, "There has never been an hour since I left the White House that I have felt a wish to return to it."

Harrison's grandson has served as Congressman from the state of Wyoming several times since 1951.

William McKinley
1897-1901

Mount McKinley, the tallest peak on the North American continent in Alaska, was named for William McKinley.

McKinley was one of the "front porch" campaigners, delivering low-key speeches from his home in Canton, Ohio. He swept into the White House with a lead of 600,000 votes.

The marriage of Ida and William McKinley had many tragedies, the worst being the death of her mother, and shortly after, the death of their new-born child. Ida suffered severe depression which developed into epilepsy, which she suffered the remainder of her life. These incidents did not alter William's love for his wife.

McKinley's campaign was the first to be conducted primarily by telephone. In this manner, he was able to contact his campaign managers in the 38 states.

McKinley is considered to be one of the kindest, most thoughtful, and most soft-spoken presidents to occupy the White House, this in spite of all the misfortune that befell his wife.

McKinley was a cigar smoker and bought them by the box, filling his pocket each morning. However, he never smoked before cameras or in the presence of his wife. He didn't want young people to see him smoke as he wished to set an example for them.

Under McKinley, the nation gained its first overseas possessions. In the 100-day war, the United States destroyed the Spanish fleet at Santiago Bay, seized Manila in the Philippines, Guam, and Puerto Rico.

While attending the Pan-American Exposition in Buffalo on September 6, 1901, he reached out to a man with a bandaged hand and was shot with two bullets from a gun concealed in the bandage. He died nine days later. His assassin was Leon Czolgoscz, a demented Czech anarchist, who was put to death 45 days later. McKinley was the third president in less than 40 years to have been assassinated in office.

At all times, President McKinley wore a lucky red carnation in his lapel. He had just given the flower to a little girl when he was shot.

McKinley joined the Masonic Lodge in Winchester, Ohio, when he was quite young and remained a member all his life.

McKinley dedicated Grant's Tomb in New York City in 1897.

McKinley's last words before he died were, "Nearer my God to Thee!"

Theodore Roosevelt
1901-1909

When Teddy Roosevelt was a young boy, he was taunted by bullies which humiliated him. Determined to build his son's body so he could defend himself, his father set up a gym for him with punching bag, bar bells, etc. This fighting spirit aided Teddy later in his life.

At the beginning of the Spanish American War, Roosevelt and his friend, Leonard Wood, rounded up sportsmen, Texas rangers, and ranchers to be trained as volunteers. The cavalry regiment became known as the "Rough Riders."

Roosevelt was escorted to his inaugural by the Rough Riders.

Not quite 43 years of age, T. R., as he was often called, was the youngest man to take the office of President.

An European visiting the United States said there were two remarkable things in the United States, Niagara Falls and Theodore Roosevelt.

For many years, Roosevelt kept secret that he was blind in his left eye, the result of a boxing match with a military aide in 1905. Because of his glasses he was called "Four Eyes," by people in the West.

Following the death of his wife and mother on the same day, Roosevelt tried to drown his grief by ranching in North Dakota. During his two-year stay in the Badlands of North Dakota, he hunted buffalo and other wild game.   He said had it not been for his experience in the Badlands, he never would have been president. Along with 206 others, he led a safari in Africa when they bagged over 500 birds, many animals, including 17 lions. He donated many of his trophies to museums.

The Roosevelts, with their six children, led a happy fun-filled life. Their boys were typical of boys of their age. At one time, Teddy had to scold the boys because they decorated a portrait of Andrew Jackson with spitballs.   The children's favorite pet was a pony named "Algonquin." When Archie was ill with the measles, Kermit and Quentin sneaked the pony up the elevator in the White House to visit him.

Teddy Roosevelt was a member of Phi Beta Kappa, national honor society at Harvard.

T. R. gave his niece, Eleanor, away when she married Franklin Roosevelt.

On a visit to a restaurant in Nashville, Tennessee, he was asked if he would like another cup of coffee. His answer, "Delightful. It's good to the last drop." Later this became the slogan for Maxwell House coffee.

Teddy was a fifth cousin of Franklin Roosevelt.

In 1908 during Roosevelt's administration, the first Model "T" was put on the market.

Roosevelt was a strong conservationist, responsible for the Reclamation Act of 1902. He doubled the number of national parks in 8 years, together with 16 national monuments and 50 game reserves.

When Roosevelt ran for the presidency in 1912, he said to his friends, "I feel as strong as a bull moose," the origin of the Bull moose party.

Legend has it that on a hunting trip, Roosevelt's guide knocked a 235-pound black bear unconscious and tied the bear to a tree. Roosevelt was summoned to shoot the bear, but he refused because the animal was captive. Cartoons concerning the incident were common and a Brooklyn couple began selling the original "teddy" bears after seeing the cartoon. Teddy bears are still a very popular item.

Roosevelt experienced several firsts in his life, among them--first president to visit every state; first president to leave the shores of our country when he went to Panama; first to invite a negro, Booker T. Washington, to the White House; first to ride in an auto; first to fly in an airplane, giving birth to the Air Force; first to play tennis; and first to win a Nobel Peace prize.

To show our strength as a nation, Roosevelt introduced a "courtesy cruise," or "great fleet," which was sent around the world to impress other powers of our increasing strength as a world power. It included 16 new battleships.

The best-known quote from Teddy Roosevelt is, "Speak softly and carry a big stick."

William Howard Taft
1909-1913

Physically, William Taft was the largest president in U. S. history, at one time weighing 330 pounds. He was 6 feet, 2 inches tall.

Taft enjoyed horseback riding as a hobby. While he was Governor of the Phillipines, he sent a cable to his good friend, Elihu Root, informing him that he had ridden his horse 25 miles through the mountains and stood it well. His friend cabled back, "How is the horse?"

"Big Lub," his nickname during high school, developed a love of baseball. He prided himself on his throwing arm. In 1908, he threw out the first ball at the opening of the baseball season, the beginning of a tradition still in effect. He also began the custom of standing up for the "seventh inning stretch."

Taft was the first president to have a car at the White House--actually he had four, a White Steamer, a Baker Electric, and two Pierce Arrows.

Mrs. Helen Taft was the first First Lady to accompany her husband in the carriage during the inaugural parade.

The slogan during Taft's presidential campaign was, "Keep on the raft with Taft."

Because of his weight, a specially made tub had to be installed in the White House; even then, the President required help to get out of the tub.

During the Taft presidency, the mayor of Tokyo, Japan, gave the city of Washington a gift of 3,000 cherry trees. Mrs. Taft was responsible for seeing that they were planted. As a result, the city celebrated the Cherry Blossom Festival annually.

Taft was the first president to appoint a woman to a governmental position, chief of the Children's Bureau, Julia Lathrop.

Mrs. Taft was a very thrifty lady. She stopped serving refreshments at the White House and eliminated catered parties. She purchased a cow, named Pauline, paid for by the government, to graze on the White House lawn.

Following his term as president, Taft received what he considered to be his greatest honor--his appointment by President Harding as Chief Justice of the Supreme Court--an office he held until his death in 1930. Taft said: "I don't remember that I was ever president."

Mrs. Taft was the first First Lady to donate her inaugural gown to the Smithsonian Institute. Since then each first lady has followed suit.

Taft was the first president to be buried in Arlington Cemetery.

Woodrow Wilson
1913-1921

Wilson, the only president to have a Ph. D. degree, served as president of Princeton University from 1902 to 1910.

The first presidential press conference was held by Woodrow Wilson on March 15, 1913.

Wilson was the last of our presidents to ride in his inaugural parade in a horse-drawn carriage.

Two of President Wilson's daughters were married in the White House six months apart.

One of the economies the White House practiced during World War I was having a herd of sheep, grazing on the White House lawn, releasing White House grounds-keepers for the war effort. In addition, the wool from the sheep was sold, raising $100,000 for the Red Cross.

Wilson was the first President to visit a European country while in office.

When the isolationists fought Wilson on the League of Nations, which they defeated, Wilson went on the road to take the problem to the people. Doctors had warned him not to take the trip, and he collapsed on his way to Wichita, Kansas. He was an invalid the rest of his life, his left side being paralyzed as a result of the stroke. He only showed his right profile to the public.

Edith Wilson is probably one of the most controversial first ladies. Many felt that after the President's stroke, she made decisions for him which affected public policy. Some called her "Mrs. President."

Despite his serious manner, Wilson had a sense of humor. He loved limericks, his favorite being, "For beauty I am not a star. There are others more handsome by far. But my face, I don't mind it because I am behind it. It's the people in front whom I jar."

Wilson was the first president to win the Nobel Peace Prize following World War I in 1919.

In August 1914, President Wilson's wife, Ellen, died. After her funeral he said, "I never understood before what a broken heart meant.."

Wilson was introduced to Mrs. Edith Galt, an attractive widow, and they became close friends, much to the delight of Washington gossip. They were married quietly in the Washington home of the widower on December 18, 1915.

Both President Wilson and his wife are buried in Washington's famous National Cathedral.

Warren G. Harding
1921-1923

Harding was a tall, handsome, genial, presidential-looking person, but he lacked firmness and "backbone." He had difficulty saying "no" to his cronies.

Before he went into politics, Harding was a newspaper editor in Marion, Ohio, where he met and married Florence Kling, rich, ambitious, and six years older than Harding. She was a very domineering wife, which probably lead to Harding's nickname for her, "The Duchess."

Harding was the first president to ride to his inauguration in an automobile--a 1921 Packard Twin.

Harding's election was the first in which women voted. He received 16,000,000 votes, twice the number other presidents had received.

At the time of Harding's victory, station KOVA, Pittsburgh, made the first radio broadcast of election returns.

When Harding became President, he brought with him to Washington many of the small-town customs of Marion, Ohio, where he had lived.

He played poker almost every night, rarely missed a ball-game, played golf often, and was extremely fond of bourbon-and-bull sessions.

Harding revived press conferences, which President Wilson had discontinued. He had excellent relations with the media, playing in some press golf matches. He had a long appointment list and supposedly saw 21 callers in a three-hour period.

Corruption was at its worst during Harding's presidency--the Teapot Dome Scandal and Veterans' Bureau being the most well known.

Harding remarked during one of these scandals, "I have no trouble with my enemies, but my friends keep me walking the floor nights."

It was said that Florence Harding, wife of the President, served as bartender at her husband's poker parties, on the second floor of the White House.

President Harding became ill with pneumonia. On August 2, 1923, Mrs. Harding was seated by his bed side, reading to him. In sleepy tones, he said, "That's good; go on," and died of a blood clot on the brain.

Death treated Harding kindly. In the months that followed, more and more scandal and corruption were reported. The American people were very disappointed and angry with the dead president, although he was never personally involved.

Many historians consider Harding to have been our worst president.

Calvin Coolidge
1923-1929

Many historians consider Coolidge the laziest president in the nation's history. During his term of office, he averaged 10 hours of sleep a day, but barely four hours of work.

Author H. L. Mencken said of Coolidge, "He slept more than any other president, whether by day or night. Nero fiddled, But Coolidge only snored."

Early in his presidency, his only hobby was walking, not so much for the exercise, as the opportunity to think. Later in his term of office, he took up the sport of fishing, at which he became relatively proficient.

At the time of the Boston Police strike, Coolidge gave one of his most famous remarks, "There is no right to strike against the public safety by anybody, any where, any time."

Coolidge lacked glamour but was very honest. He was a man of few words, giving him the nickname "Silent Cal."

Coolidge was a very frugal person, reputed to have saved $50,000 from his salary of $75,000.

Coolidge took complete charge of the household and checked everything. He would not let his wife drive a car, she could not wear slacks, and he demanded to know where she was every minute of the day. Cal loved his wife very much but had difficulty expressing it.

After the news of Harding's death, Coolidge was sworn in as President by his father, a notary public, at 3 a.m. in a lamp-lit sitting room, after which it is said Calvin went back to sleep. He took the oath of office a second time in Washington from a Justice of the Supreme Court on August 21.

The custom of Christmas tree lighting on the White House lawn was begun by Coolidge.

Coolidge's inaugural address was the first to be heard over radio.

It is reported that President Coolidge wore gloves while fishing and that someone baited his hook.

Coolidge never seemed fond of his successor, Herbert Hoover, and stated, "That man has offered me unsolicited advice for six years--all of it bad."

Grace Coolidge had to be a good hostess to compensate for her husband's lack of conversation. She was an excellent conversationalist and enjoyed telling stories about her husband.

After becoming president, Coolidge joined the Congregational Church, his first church membership.

Will Rogers, famous humorist, once said of Coolidge, "He never told jokes but had more subtle humor than any man I have ever met."

When Coolidge lived in the White House, he enjoyed pressing a buzzer to keep the staff on its toes; then he disappeared.

At a dinner party, the hostess said to President Coolidge, "I made a bet that I could get you to say more than two words." Coolidge replied, "You lose."

Following a church service, Mrs. Coolidge is reported to have asked her husband what the minister said about sin. The President replied, "He was against it."

As it was widely known that Coolidge slept a great deal of the time, when he died, H. L. Mencken remarked, "How can they tell?"

One of his shortest, most famous quotes is, "I do not choose to run for President in 1928."

Al Smith, a one-time presidential candidate, asked Coolidge how he was able to talk so little. His reply was, "I've discovered that the average man can tell all he knows in ten minutes, so why interrupt him!"

Another interesting anecdote tells about Coolidge fishing and when he lost the fish, he said, "DAMN!" Then he turned to his fishing friend and said in a sly way, "Guess I'm a real fisherman now; I cussed."

Coolidge smoked cigars which cost him 21 cents each; however, he gave his guests cigars which cost 5 cents.

Herbert Hoover
1929-1933

Hoover was born in West Branch, Iowa, of poor parents, both of whom died before he was ten. He was sent to Oregon to live with an uncle whose son had died. 78 years later, Herbert Hoover recalled, "The only material assets which I had were two dimes in my pocket, the suit of clothes that I wore, and I had some extra underpinnings provided by loving aunts."

The Hoover family were Quakers, and the mother often spoke before Quaker worshipers in the one-room school house built in 1853.

Hoover made his fortune as a mining engineer, who gained an international reputation as a "doctor of sick mines."

Hoover was a member of the first graduating class at Stanford University in 1895, with a degree in engineering.

Hoover loved to fish and was called the "stylish angler."

At age 24, Hoover was sent to China as a mining engineer. While there, he sent a cablegram to Lou Henry, whom he met in a geologist's laboratory at Stanford, asking her to marry him. She consented and Hoover made a quick trip to California for the wedding. They honeymooned on their way to his new job in China.

The Hoovers lived in London from 1902 to 1917, where both their sons were born.

In October 1914, as Hoover was about to leave England for America, the American ambassador asked him to help the people of Brussels, Belgium, who were on the verge of starvation. He formed the Commission for Relief of Belgium, which during four years fed eleven million people of Helgium and northern France.

At home, Hoover became U. S. Food administrator for President Wilson. After the war, Hoover continued to help feed a hungry world. The fact that his methods were so efficient enabled him to be successful in these areas.

By 1914, the poor boy from Iowa had become a millionaire with a chain of offices around the globe.

Both Democrats and Republicans wanted him as a candidate, but he ran as a Republican and defeated Alfred E. Smith by the largest popular and electoral vote received by a candidate up to that time.

Hoover paid his own expenses during his relief operations, and he never used his $75,000 presidential salary.

Mrs. Hoover served as National President of the Girl Scouts of America in 1922 and again in 1935.

President Hoover signed an Act of Congress in 1931 making The Star-Spangled Banner the national anthem.

Eight months after Hoover's election, the nation experienced Black Thursday, when the stock market crashed on Wall Street. With the beginning of the great depression, the word "Hoover" was applied to

Harry S. Truman
1945-1953

Truman's middle initial "S." doesn't stand for any thing. He had two grandfathers--one's middle name was Shippe and the other Solomon. Not wanting to show favoritism, the parents gave him just the middle initial.

Truman was the only president that did not have a college education.

Truman was a prolific reader and says that he gained much of his knowledge from long hours in the library studying the encyclopedia. His favorite book was the Bible, naming The Sermon on The Mount its greatest part. After the Bible, his favorite author was Shakespeare.

Truman was considered to be a very good pianist. He stated that if he had been a good pianist, he would have never been the President.

In 1921, with the imminent financial failure of his haberdashery shop, Truman turned to politics.

His marriage to Bess Truman is one of the most devoted of all the presidents. She exerted a great deal of influence over her husband, and he often introduced her in this manner: "Meet the Boss."

Their only child, Margaret, was the pride and joy of both Harry and Bess. He taught her how to play the piano, and she became a concert pianist. Following her first formal Washington concert, a music critic for the Washington Post severely criticized Miss Truman's playing. Harry was furious and wrote Hume, the critic, a letter in which he called him "a frustrated old man who never made a success, an eight-ulcer man on a four-ulcer job, and all four ulcers working." In haste, he mailed the letter which the Post published, causing the President much embarrassment.

Once while campaigning from a train, Mr. Truman came out on the platform in his pajamas.

Truman was the last president to serve before television became popular. He did appear on television once to encourage people to vote.

Truman was the last president to have a Secretary of War and the first to have a Secretary of Defense.

When discussing Eisenhower's intelligence, Truman said, "The General doesn't know any more about politics than a pig knows about Sunday."

Truman's favorite foods were tuna and noodle casserole, meat loaf, and Ozark pudding, making him a "true man of the people."

Truman's inauguration was the first to be covered by television.

On their 50th wedding anniversary, Harry said, "Three things can ruin a husband--money, power, and women. I never had money. I never wanted power, and the only woman in my life is sitting beside me right now."

When President Truman went for his daily walk, he always carried a cane, which he did not need.

When he retired, he could display 150 canes, gifts from his many admirers all over the United States.

Truman kept two mottos on his desk: "The buck stops here," and a quote from Mark Twain, "Always do right. This will gratify some people and astonish the rest."

Truman once said that no man should ever commercialize the presidency; he declined many business offers after leaving the White House. When his memoirs were published, some 500 friends, mostly officeholders, asked for free copies. The publisher, Doubleday, offered to give him an extra 500 free, but he refused, insisting that he be billed.

The Trumans lived in Blair House for three years while the White House was being renovated. While there, a Puerto Rican planned to murder the President, but his attempt failed; however, one guard was killed and two wounded. The would-be assassin was captured and executed.

After the death of Franklin Roosevelt, Mr. Truman asked Mrs. Roosevelt if there was anything he could do for her. Her reply was, "Is there anything we can do for you, for you are the one in trouble now."

When asked what he did first on his return home to Independence, at the end of his presidential term, he said, "I took the suitcases to the attic."

Dwight Eisenhower
1953-1961

Eisenhower was graduated from West Point in 1911, in the top one-third of his class.

Eisenhower was an avid golfer, and if time allowed, he would play twice a day. Some of his critics felt he spent too much time playing golf. Auto stickers appeared, bearing the motto, "Ben Hogan for President. If we're going to have a golfer, let's have a good one."

Eisenhower's cabinet was referred to as nine millionaires and one plumber, the latter being Secretary of Labor Martin Durkin, who was also head of the plumber's union.

Mamie Eisenhower never voted in a presidential election until her husband ran for office.

Eisenhower, who was very bald, once said to his balding secretary, George Humphrey, "I see you part your hair like I do."

Eisenhower was considered to be the best prepared person in foreign affairs to ever be elected to the presidency; he was considered a master in international politics.

Because of their years of association with the Army, the Eisenhowers gave lavish state dinners, consisting of many courses of gourmet types of food. However the President enjoyed dinner on trays with a few friends to watch a movie or play bridge.

The Eisenhowers almost moved out of the White House, as he wanted to live in a high-rise, where most other generals lived.

Eisenhower was once asked by reporters what major decision Nixon had participated in and he replied, "If you give me a week, I may think of one."

When Eisenhower became president and began using FDR's mountain retreat which he called "Shangri-la," Ike changed the name to "Camp David," saying "Shangri-la is just a little too fancy for a Kansas farm boy."

President Eisenhower was the first president to use makeup for his TV appearances, the application of which was supervised by his actor friend, Robert Montgomery.

Alice Roosevelt Longworth, TR's daughter, was very outspoken, particularly where occupants of the White House were concerned. Of Eisenhower, she said, "A nice boob."

At the conclusion of the war, Eisenhower received Russia's Order of Victory, the first time a foreigner had ever won the medal.

From 1948 to 1950 Eisenhower was president of Columbia University. At one dinner he was to be the last of several speakers, all of whom gave long talks. It was so late when Ike's turn came that he discarded his prepared talk and reminded his audience that every speech, written or otherwise, had to have punctuation. "Tonight," he said, "I am the punctuation--the period," and sat down. He said later it was one of his most popular speeches.

Eisenhower held the first televised press conference on January 19, 1955.

Known at West Point as the "Kansas Cyclone" for his football skills, Ike might have become a pro football player if he hadn't injured a knee tackling the great Jim Thorpe.

Accomplishments during Eisenhower's two administrations are: Air Force Academy and the Department of Health, Education, and Welfare were created; the minimum wage was raised to a dollar an hour; two civil rights bills were passed; Social Security was expanded; the St. Lawrence seaway project was authorized and completed.

Known as the father of the Interstate Highway System, one sees signs along highways saying, "Dwight D. Eisenhower Highway System." The first such sign was placed in Kansas because Eisenhower's family had lived in Abilene.

Mamie and Ike celebrated their 52nd wedding anniversary before his death.

When Ike left the presidency, he and Mamie retired to their farm in Gettysburg, Pennsylvania, which is not too far from the famous battlefield.

John F. Kennedy 1961-1963

John Kennedy was the only president awarded the Pulitzer Prize for Literature for his work, "Profiles in Courage," written in 1957.

In 1946, when he was 29 years old, Kennedy won his first political office, that of Representative. Because of his youth, he was often mistakenly taken for an elevator operator.

During his term as Representative in 1946, Kennedy was critical of his fellow members and said, "The House is run by a crowd of old men who would have been pensioned off years ago if they were in private industry."

On September 12, 1953, while he was in the Senate, he married beautiful Jacqueline Bouvier at a glittering ceremony in Newport, Rhode Island.

Kennedy was the first president to have both his parents in attendance at his inauguration.

Pierre Salinger, President Kennedy's press secretary and friend, says that Jackie Kennedy hated the term "First Lady," saying it was presumptuous, as it was her husband that had been elected to the presidency; she hadn't been elected to anything.

JFK was the first graduate of the Naval Academy at Annapolis to become president.

Kennedy's famous quote from his inaugural address, "Ask not what your country can do for you; ask what you can do for your country," was first spoken by Oliver Wendell Holmes, an American writer and father of Chief Justice Oliver Wendell Holmes, Jr., on May 31, 1884. His exact words were, "Recall what our country has done for each of us and ask ourselves what we can do for our country in return."

President Kennedy made the bareheaded look acceptable with his bareheaded Inauguration in 1961, much to the amazement of many people. During the '60s and '70s the men's hat industry was almost dead because of this event.

On John F. Kennedy's 21st birthday, his gift from his father was a $1,000,000 trust fund.

In a reply during the 1960 presidential campaign to a question about his Catholicism and views on separation of church and state, he said, "If a president breaks his oath, he is not only committing a crime against the Constitution, for which the Congress can and should impeach him, but he is committing a sin against his God."

John F. Kennedy, born at home (83 Beals St. in Brookline, Mass.) on May 29, 1917, was the first President to have been born in the 20th century.

Jackie Kennedy was the youngest First Lady of the 20th century.

Historian James MacGregor Burns, consultant to JFK, says of him, "He was the last president who made the American people feel that government was good or could be good. His concern with freedom, democracy, liberty--those great values, those great symbols--that lives on in our memory."

Kennedy became the first Catholic to be elected President of the United States. He was also the youngest person ever to be elected to this office.

Feelings between President Kennedy and his Vice President, Lyndon Johnson, were not always the best. When Kennedy was composing a birthday telegram to his second in command as a goodwill gesture, he said, "This is worse than drafting a state document."

President Kennedy was the first president to have been a Boy Scout.

Kennedy was the first president to donate his salary to charity.

Kennedy was responsible for the introduction of the Peace Corps.

Kennedy's term of office lasted only 1,037 days.

In November, 1983, 20 years after Kennedy's assassination, he was still voted the favorite of all presidents, according to a Newsweek poll.

Kennedy's administration was called the "New Frontier."

Lyndon B. Johnson
1963-1969

Lyndon Johnson was the first member of Congress to go on active military duty in World War II.

At 44, Johnson was the youngest man ever to be elected to the position of floor leader of the Senate by either party.

Johnson was the second tallest president, being 6 feet, 3 inches; Lincoln was one inch taller.

When President Johnson thought well of a person, he would say, "He's a good man to go to the well with."

LBJ appointed the first black person to be a cabinet member--Robert Weaver, administrator of the Department of Housing and Urban Development.

President Johnson had a sign on his desk which read, "If you're talking, you're not learning."

Johnson applied the phrase, "Great Society," to his presidential term. Johnson married Claudia Taylor of San Antonio, Texas, the daughter of a wealthy East Texas landowner in 1937. Her wealth did not stop LBJ from using a $2 wedding band when they were married, as this was all he could afford.

Since early childhood, Mrs. Johnson had been called "Lady Bird," because the family cook said she was "pretty as a lady bird."

With Lyndon Johnson, there was no doubt as to who was in charge. He told a member of his staff, "Just you remember this, there's only two kinds at the White House. There's elephants and there's ants. And I'm the only elephant."

Lady Bird Johnson was the first woman to hold the Bible when her husband was sworn in as Vice-President.

After 23 years as a member of Congress and almost three years as Vice-President, Johnson was considered to be one of the most politically experienced men to hold the office of President.

Vice-President Johnson took the oath of office to become president aboard Air Force One, following President Kennedy's assassination. Sarah T. Hughes administered the oath.

LBJ possessed boundless energy--in one day in the campaign of 1964 he gave 24 speeches; also in 1968 he visited and gave speeches in five Central American countries in one day.

Johnson enjoyed controlling people; insiders say that he treated Vice-president Humphrey like a servant.

There was much feminine activity in the White House during the Johnson administration. Both daughters were married during the five years Johnson was President, having large Washington weddings.

Lady Bird was considered to be one of the hardest working first ladies; largely because of her, Congress passed a National Beautification Act.

The Vietnam War was considered to be his downfall. He was caught in the middle between the battle of the Hawks and Doves. Violence broke out at home with student uprisings and black riots.

The first Civil Rights Act was passed in 1964 during Johnson's administration; in fact, he was responsible for passage of the greatest group of Civil Rights laws in U. S. history.

One day in 1966, Johnson turned to Lady Bird and said, "I can't get out. I can't finish it with what I've got, So what the hell can I do?" This frustration ended in his decision not to run for reelection in 1968.

After leaving the presidency, LBJ lived quietly at his beloved ranch near Johnson City, Texas. While there, he said, "All my life I have drawn sustenance from the river and hills of my native state. I want no less for all the children of America than what I was privileged to have as a boy."

All members of the Johnson family have the same initials, L.B.J. The president said, "It's cheaper this way, because we can all use the same luggage."

One of Johnson's often repeated statements, a quote from the Bible was "Come, let us reason together."

Richard M. Nixon
1969-1974

Richard Nixon was raised a Quaker and often in his youth would attend church four times on Sunday.

Nixon was class president and second in his class at Whittier College in California. He was a champion debater, his ability well displayed in his television debates with John F. Kennedy during the presidential campaign.

While acting in an amateur theater group, he met Pat Ryan, a high school typing teacher, whom he married on June 21, 1940.

In 1950, at age 37, he became the youngest Republican U. S. Senator.

Nixon began his climb to the presidency by answering this ad, "Congressman Wanted."

Three days before Nixon's inauguration in 1970, the president's salary was raised to $200,000.

Nixon earned ten battle stars for his service duty. As Lieutenant Commander in the Navy, he was called "The Gentle Tiger" by his colleagues.

Nixon is the only president to have his name placed on a plaque on the moon. Following the landing on the moon, President Nixon said, "This has been the greatest week in history."

Nixon's daughter, Tricia, was the first member of a president's family to have an outdoor wedding at the White House, which was a lavish affair since the Nixon's enjoyed entertaining in that manner.

Football was of great interest to Richard Nixon when he attended Whittier College. He tried out for the team, but weighing only 150 pounds, he was at a disadvantage. A former football star who played on the same team as Nixon said he was a lousy football player but had lots of "guts." He was so eager to play that he was invariably offside, drawing a penalty.

Experts feel that, had there been no debates in 1964, Nixon would have won the election. His personal appearance on television was not good compared to Kennedy.

In 1972, President Nixon flew to Peking, China, to confer with leaders, becoming the first President to visit this country. He also was the first President to visit the Soviet Union.

Nixon is the only person to have been elected to the Vice-Presidency twice and to the Presidency twice.

Nixon described himself as an "introvert in an extrovert's profession."

The Watergate scandal ended the practice of taping White House conversations, which had been happening long before Nixon's involvement. Aides insist that no president since Nixon, including Ronald Reagan, has made secret tapes.

Vice-president Nixon stayed at the Leamington Hotel in Minneapolis when he was Grand Marshal of the Aquatennial Parade in 1968.

In 1972, Nixon's wife, Pat, traveled to three African nations as a personal representative of the President--the first time an American First Lady had visited these countries.

While in service in the Navy, Nixon learned to be a shrewd poker player. It is said that he once bluffed a Lieutenant Commander with a pair of deuces, costing his opponent, $1,500.

The Nixon library opened July 19, 1990 in Yorba Linda, California, at a cost of $21,000,000 privately-raised dollars, including $2,000,000 given by Nixon himself. The library is privately funded.

On the occasion of his 75th birthday, Mrs. Nixon said, "My husband does not dwell on the past. He is a positive thinker and an optimist. He has a very good mind, a big heart, and a kind soul."

Richard Nixon was the first president to resign from office.

Nixon appointed Gerald Ford as Vice-President, after Spiro Agnew's resignation, on October 10, 1973.

Due to the Watergate scandal, Nixon lost all opportunity to rate as a "good" president.

Gerald Ford
1974-1977

Gerald Ford was the first President not elected to the vice-presidency or the presidency by American voters. In October, 1973, Vice-President Spiro Agnew resigned, and President Nixon appointed Gerald Ford to fill the office. Less than eight months later, Ford became the 38th president, following Nixon's resignation.

In 1934, while attending Michigan University, he was voted its most valuable player.

Ford was born Leslie Lynch King, but shortly there after his parents were divorced. When he was two, his mother married Gerald R. Ford, a Grand Rapids paint salesman, who adopted Leslie and gave him the name Gerald Rudolf Ford, Jr.

When Gerald Ford was 23, he spent the summer as a forest ranger at Yellowstone National Park. His good looks landed him jobs as a male model, and his face was on the cover of Look and Cosmopolitan.

Ford joined the Navy in 1942 and achieved the rank of Lieutenant Commander; he left the Navy in 1946 with ten battle stars.

Elizabeth Bloomer Warren, a former Martha Graham dancer and Powers model, became Mrs. Gerald Ford on October 15, 1948.

Being a very frugal individual, President Ford was careful about turning off lights both in the White House and at the office. He antagonized his staff by using pencils until they were tiny stubs.

President Ford is an avid golfer. Of his golf game, Bob Hope said jokingly, "His fame as an erratic hitter is richly deserved. He doesn't really have to keep score. He can just look back and count the walking wounded."

The Fords were the exception to the rule that Presidents and First Ladies did not sleep in the same room, due to different schedules, late phone calls, etc. Betty Ford said, "We've slept in the same bed for 25 years, and I see no reason to change now."

Lyndon Johnson made the following observation about Ford: "The trouble with Jerry Ford is he can't walk and chew gum at the same time."

At the time of their marriage, Ford was a Congressman from Michigan. He rose quickly up the congressional ladder, and in January, 1965, was voted Minority Leader.

Gerald Ford is the only President who had an opportunity to play professional football; he was drafted by the Green Bay Packers.

Even though he was a Republican, Ford had a portrait of Harry Truman hung in the Cabinet Room and placed a bust of Mr. Truman near his desk in the Oval Office.

The Fords had their own style of entertaining, typified by the dinner they gave for Queen Elizabeth and Prince Phillip in July 1976. A huge tent was erected in the Rose Garden, and the first course was New England lobster.

Ford was the president who did the most exercising, swimming 30 minutes every night before dinner. Then he was ready for braised pork chops with a little red wine in cabbage.

Ford and Coolidge were the only 20th century presidents who were sworn in to office in August.

President Ford says that when he took office after Richard Nixon's resignation because of the Watergate scandal, he had to spend one-fourth of his time contending with questions about Nixon. "The only way to clear the decks was to grant that pardon and get the problem out of the Oval Office," said Ford.

When Gerald Ford walked into President Nixon's Oval Office, the latter said, "You will do a good job, Jerry." This told Ford that the president was going to resign his office.

President Ford says he cried in the Oval Office when doctors told him that his wife had breast cancer. He called it "the lowest and loneliest moment" in his 895-day presidency.

On the loss of his election, Ford said, "No one likes to lose, but it isn't the end of the world."

James E. Carter
1977-1981

Plains, Georgia, the birthplace of Jimmy Carter, became a famous tourist spot during his presidency. It is a very small town with many antique shops.

Jimmy grew up on the family farm, where the family raised most of their own food, using mules for cultivation. There was no electricity or indoor plumbing when Jimmy was in his teens.

President Carter was graduated from the Naval Academy in 1940 with honors, 59th in a class of 820.

Carter's military career was cut short by the death of his father in 1953, when he returned to Plains to run the family business, Carter Farms, Inc., seed peanuts being the primary product.

Shortly after his graduation from the Naval Academy, he married Rosalynn Smith, a childhood neighbor.

Carter was the first person to be elected from the deep South in the 20th century.

As Governor of Georgia, Mr. Carter placed the portrait of Martin Luther King in the State Capitol, where only portraits of whites had previously hung.

Jimmy Carter was the only president to have been a commander of a submarine, having been hand picked by Admiral Rickover for duty in the new nuclear submarine force.

As a matter of personal principle, Carter believes that, as a former U. S. President, he should not sit on any corporation boards and has refused all such offers.

The sweater Jimmy Carter wore in his first fireside chat as president, in February 1977--a plain tan cardigan--hangs in a small display case in the museum of the Carter Presidential Center in Atlanta.

Before her husband's election, when asked what he had that President Ford had not, she replied, "He has me." She turned out to be probably the most powerful and influential first lady in history.

Since leaving the White House, Carter has worked to improve Third World health and agriculture in Ethiopia and Sudan, has monitored elections in Nicaragua, Panama, Haiti, and the Dominican Republic, and privately builds houses for the poor worldwide with Habitat for Humanity. He recently was awarded the 1991 Physicians for Social Responsibility Award for his "commitment to peace and human dignity."

It was President Carter who pardoned about 10,000 Vietnam draft evaders.

Rosalyn Carter's biggest disappointment while her husband was president was the fact that the Equal Rights Amendment did not pass.

Jimmy Carter came into the national political limelight in 1963 as a result of his liberal attitude on racial issues. As a Deacon of the Plains Baptist Church, Jimmy voted not to exclude negroes as members of the church.

President Carter wished to be a "man of the people." He had the most informal inauguration since Andrew Jackson; he wore a business suit; when he gave his oath of office, he gave his name as "Jimmy Carter," rather than "James Earl Carter." Following the inauguration, he and his wife walked the distance down Pennsylvania Avenue to the White House.

Carter was extremely intelligent; in fact, it is said that while in college the only time he opened a book was when classmates desired help. Historians felt he brought a greater knowledge of political science to the presidency than any other president, except possibly Woodrow Wilson.

One of Carter's famous sayings is, "The only title in our democracy superior to that of president is the title of citizen."

Rosalynn Carter learned her husband's business at his side. She kept the books at the peanut warehouse and she kept the books on political supporters. In June 1977 she became a special envoy to Latin America, surprising the heads of state with her knowledge of matters of substance. In the second year of her husband's presidency, she began attending Cabinet meetings.

President Carter appointed the first black to the position of U. S. Ambassador to the United Nations, namely Andrew Young, who later became mayor of the city of Atlanta.

Ronald Reagan
1981-1989

Concerning his boyhood, President Reagan said his family was poor but didn't know it at the time. He remarked that "while they didn't live exactly on the wrong side of the tracks, at times they could hear the train whistle."

Reagan is only the second Irishman to become President. He was a true descendant of poor Irish Catholics who came to this country at the time of the potato famine in 1840.

Not only was Reagan the first screen star to be elected President, he also was the first to have been divorced. For over 200 years, there was a political belief that a divorced person could never win the office of President. As an actor in his early life, he appeared in 51 movies, the most famous of which was "Knute Rockne," in which he played "Gipper."

Reagan once said in 1982, that "you feel like a bird in a gilded cage in the White House."

In 1985, the Reagans sent out 200,000 Christmas cards.

President Reagan's first inaugural celebration was the biggest and most extravagant ever, costing $16.3 million, making it the most expensive inaugural in the nation's history.

Reagan was elected to public office four times-twice as Governor of California and twice as President. Of his Sacramento period, he said, "For eight years, somebody handed me a piece of paper every night that told me what I was going to be doing the next day."

While attending Drake University in DesMoines, Iowa, President Reagan was a disc jockey at station WHO in that city.

Ronald Reagan is the only president to be elected to the Sports Casters and Sports Writers Hall of Fame.

Reagan is reported to have said that being in the White House gave him claustrophobia, and he confided in a friend that "he wished to hell that he could run the country from California."

In tiny Tampico, Illinois, (1,000 population) where Reagan was born, there is one lonely gas station that pumps "Ronnie regular," and "Nancy no lead."

President Reagan wears a hearing aid in each ear. His hearing problem began years ago, when, on a movie set, a fellow actor fired a .38 too close to his head.

Former Speaker of the House, Tip O'Neill, remarked that he liked Reagan, but that he was the laziest president in history.

Ronald Reagan was the first president to enjoy two terms of office sin#e Eisenhower held the office.

President Reagan's chief means of relaxation is horseback riding. Another hobby is wood chopping. He is probably the best known wood-chopping President since Abraham Lincoln. He also enjoys helping the foreman of his ranch mend fences.

Reagan was the first president to hold his inauguration ceremony at the west end of the Capitol. The event was covered by a multi-million dollar insurance package that covered over 500 automobiles used in the parade, losses of souvenir sales, spectator stands, etc. The day was the coldest on record for inaugurals--10 degrees and a windchill of minus 25 degrees.

Following the attempted assassination on President Reagan, Nancy and he no longer attended regular church services, not wishing to have to subject the congregation to all the necessary security measures.

While President, Reagan removed the portrait of President Truman from the Cabinet Room and replaced it with a portrait of President Coolidge, because Mr. Reagan admired Coolidge for his character traits of integrity, thrift, and hard work.

At the time of his inauguration, Reagan was 69 years old; in contrast, Teddy Roosevelt was 42 when he took the oath of office.

Reagan's effective use of television in presenting the administration's program earned him the nickname of "The Great Communicator."

Known for his quick wit, President Reagan has been quoted as saying, "One of the better jobs I have had in my entire life, while working my way through Eureka College, was washing dishes in the girl's dormitory."

One of his most famous statements followed the attempt on his life, when he said to his wife, Nancy, "Honey, I forgot to duck."

When Reagan kicked the smoking habit, he turned to jelly beans. 7,000 pounds of this candy were shipped to Washington at the time of his inauguration, valued at $28,000. For this occasion, the jelly beans were red, white, and blue in color.

After recovering from his attempted assassination, President Reagan remarked, "If I had had this much attention in Hollywood, I would have stayed there."

Reagan's ideal politician was Franklin Delano Roosevelt; in fact, during his early years, Mr. Reagan was a Democrat.

While President Reagan was hospitalized after the attempt on his life, it is said he remarked to a nurse, "Does Nancy know about us?" At this same time, he also remarked that the assassin "ruined one of my best suits."

When the Reagans entered the White House, Mrs. Reagan spent $209,000 for Lenox china, for which she was severely criticized. Later it was made known that the taxpayer hadn't paid for the china, but that it was paid for by private donations.

Another statement from Reagan--"If we doubled or tripled our troubles, we'd still be better off than any other country on earth."

As President of the Screen Actors' Guild, Reagan was the first U. S. President to serve as a labor union leader.

In response to the many who criticized Reagan's age to serve as President, he asked this question, "How old would you be if you didn't know how old you were?"

President Reagan's nickname for his wife, Nancy, is "Pee Wee Powerhouse."

It is reported that Reagan never looked at the front page of the newspaper until he had read the comics.

On President Reagan's first working day at the Oval Office, the Marine Band gave him a short serenade. He beamed and said, "This is great. I wish you could come and play for me every morning."

Reagan's White House tenure has been anything but easy. He has been shot, had major cancer surgery, suffered through his wife's cancer operation and experienced myriad setbacks that would have doomed other leaders. Preparing for his waning days of office, Reagan said, "As they say in showbiz, let's bring them to their feet with our closing act."

On the occasion of his 75th birthday, to a gathering at the Treasury Department he said he preferred to think of his birthday as the 36th anniversary of my 39th birthday. A few more of these and I'll be just about due for a mid-life crisis."

Another comic statement from Reagan while he was hospitalized--he said to the doctors surrounding him, "Please tell me that you are all Republicans."

One of Reagan's last acts as President was to send a "thank you" note to Margaret Thatcher, Prime Minister of England.

George Bush
1989-

Prescott Bush, the father of George Bush, was a United States Senator from Connecticut for ten years and was the greatest influence in the life of his son.

President Bush played golf in his youth, but because it was so time-consuming, he gave it up for tennis, which remains the family's favorite recreation.

George Bush is the only President who previously served as the representative to the United Nations.

Bush calls the inauguration ceremony, "an exhaustive and inhumane process," lasting five days, ending at Washington Cathedral with the National Day of Prayer and Thanksgiving service.

Since George Bush has been president, every Cabinet meeting is opened with a prayer.

Barbara Bush's hair turned white in her early 30s.

White House Correspondents refer to the President, who is hyperactive, as "the Mexican Jumping Bean," and because of her white hair, Barbara is called "the Silver Fox."

In remarks to workers at the United Electric Controls factory in suburban Boston, First Lady Barbara said, "I've stayed happily married for 46 years because I've stayed out of my husband's business."

George Bush is the only president to have met with the Dali Lama, because up to this time the Chinese felt that such a meeting would be meddling.

Guests at the White House find all the "extras" of a first class hotel-- heavy terry cloth robes in the bathrooms, stationery engraved with "The President's House" on the desk, and fresh flowers everywhere.

President Bush arises at an early hour (prior to 6 a.m.), reads the morning papers in bed, clipping and underscoring items that are of special interest to him. He arrives at the Oval Office each morning with an armful of thank-you notes, typed the night before in his hunt-and-peck method.

Of all the nation's presidents, George Bush and wife, Barbara, are considered to be the most generous in inviting guests to stay, not only at the White House, but also the home at Kennebunkport. The Bush family has been spending summers here since 1880. President Bush says this is his favorite place on earth, "Politics be damned!"

At age 66, George Bush is learning how to use a computer. He is still a two-finger typist on the personal computer that he had installed in the Oval Office.

Following graduation from Yale in the late '40s, Bush and Barbara (married January 6, 1945) went to Texas where his first job was with Dresser Industries in Odessa. His duties were custodial, sweeping out warehouses and painting oil drilling machinery at $375 a month.

The first tragedy in the life of George and Barbara Bush was the death of their daughter, Robin, at age four of leukemia. This developed in George a resolve to serve others during his lifetime.

Toward the end of January 1975, Bush was confirmed as director of the Central Intelligence Agency; he called it the most exciting facet of ten years of public service. He left the agency in 1977.

While offering a chair to a lady, President Bush is reported to have said, "Chivalry is only reasonably dead."

Bush will rank with the four tallest presidents, behind Lincoln, Lyndon Johnson, and Jefferson; he is also one of four left-handed presidents, the others being Garfield, Truman, and Ford.

Mrs. Bush is one of the most prolific writers of thank-you notes in White House history, and her husband is always quick to visit a sick friend or to invite a new friend to their house in Maine.

While attending Yale, George Bush was captain and played first base on the baseball team.

During the first two years of his term of office, Bush logged more than 275,000 miles to 28 foreign countries and 45 of the 50 states.

The presidential inauguration of George Bush represented the bicentennial of that ceremony, and in some ways resembled that of George Washington 200 years ago; for example, Bush was sworn in with the same Bible, held by his wife, Barbara; the archway of the door to the West Front, where the president-elect and vice-president-elect entered was draped in red bunting similar to that used in 1789; two flags with 13 stars representing the original 13 states were part of the backdrop, together with two 38-star flags from 1889 and the 50 state flag.

The largest contingent of family ever to attend an inaugural was that of George Bush--almost 240 were in attendance.

The desk in the Oval Office which George Bush uses daily is the same as that used by Franklin Delano Roosevelt, John F. Kennedy, and Ronald Reagan. It is made from an Old English sailing boat, a gift from Queen Victoria.

In 1943, Bush became a newly commissioned ensign and was the youngest pilot in the United States Navy.

On February 2, 1944, George's plane was hit and the aircraft was set on fire. He was rescued by a submarine. Later he was awarded the Distinguished Flying Cross and three air medals.

Two months after Bush's discharge from the Navy in September 1945, he joined the largest ever freshman class at Yale--8,000, of whom, 5,000 were servicemen.

George Bush is a parishioner and former vestryman of St. Martin's Episcopal Church in Houston and a vestry man at St. Ann's at Kennebunkport.

Unlike most presidents in recent years, President Bush enjoys eating out about once a month, the Peking Gourmet Inn in Falls Church, Virginia, being one of his favorite places. Secret Service agents and police are everywhere. The President sits at a big round table in a partitioned area that has a bullet-proof window, installed by the restaurant owners.

President Bush is considered to be an "above average" tipper--20 per cent.

George Bush is the first modern president to veto a civil rights bill.

Explaining why he doesn't play golf with his wife, Barbara, President Bush says, "We're going down life's path hand in hand for many years, but in golf we go our separate ways."

George Bush, the 43rd vice-president, is only the fourth elected to succeed the president he served, and the first to do so since 1837. The others were Martin Van Buren succeeded Andrew Jackson in

1837; Thomas Jefferson succeeded John Adams in 1801; John Adams succeeded George Washington in 1797.

Speaking of the 200th birthday of the cornerstone laying of the White House on October 13, 1792, Barbara Bush says, "I am thrilled that George and I will be living here when the White House celebrates its 200th birthday next year. It is ironic that we can't find the cornerstone. Everyone knows it is here somewhere, because there are written accounts of the ceremony in 1792."

Each Christmas Barbara Bush continues a ceremonial she began in 1981 as the vice-president's wife-placing the main ornament atop the National Christmas tree.

PRESIDENTIAL RATING

One of the fascinating subjects that I encountered while researching for this book was the many ratings of our presidents, by college professors, historians, and lay people like myself. The first of these ratings was published in the early 40s, and there have been many since that time. Therefore, I decided to follow suit and present my own ratings.

You may wonder why I have placed George Washington first in the "great" category. In my research I discovered that most evaluators place Washington in the "great" group, but not necessarily first. My thinking this is that if it weren't for Washington, there wouldn't be any United States of America.

Do you agree?

The following represent my personal rating:

GREAT PRESIDENTS:
George Washington
Abraham Lincoln
Franklin Delano Roosevelt
Thomas Jefferson
Theodore Roosevelt

NEAR-GREAT PRESIDENTS:
Woodrow Wilson
Andrew Jackson
Harry Truman
James Polk
John Adams

ABOVE-AVERAGE PRESIDENTS:
John Quincy Adams
James Madison
James Monroe
Grover Cleveland
Ronald Reagan
Lyndon Johnson
John Kennedy

PRESIDENTIAL RATING (continued)

AVERAGE PRESIDENTS:

William Taft
Martin Van Buren
Herbert Hoover
William McKinley
Rutherford Hayes
Chester Arthur
John Tyler
Gerald Ford
James Carter
Dwight Eisenhower
Benjamin Harrison

BELOW-AVERAGE PRESIDENTS:

Calvin Coolidge
Franklin Pierce

FAILURES:

Andrew Johnson
Richard Nixon
 (because of Watergate)
Ulysses S. Grant
Warren Harding
Millard Fillmore
James Buchanan

James Garfield, William Henry Harrison, and Zachary Taylor are not included in my ratings because neither were in office long enough to pass judgment on their ability.